MW00476637

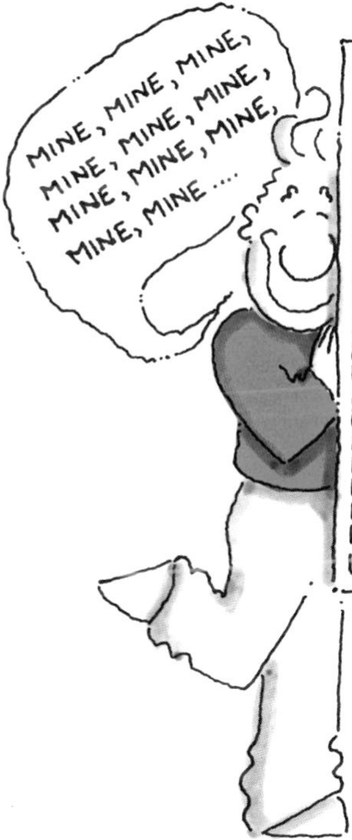


THIS BOOK **BELONGS** TO:

NAME ______________________________

DATE ______________________________

"Lucky"

Graphics and design by Deborah Henckel and Jennifer Gaul
Cover by Robert Bucciarelli Design, San Diego, CA

# SAY WHAT?

The 305 Best Things Ever Said
About Service, Sales, and Supervision

# FOREWORD

This book is a collection of quotes from the archives of Pencom, Inc., a company that specializes in training and consulting for sales, service, marketing and management worldwide. Pencom's clients include Anheuser-Busch, Inc., Marriott Hotels, Visa USA and over 100,000 other successful companies. For more information about Pencom call 1-800-247-8514. Thank you.

# INTRODUCTION

Trying to compile a collection of the 305 very best service, sales and management quotes into one volume is a lot like being a mosquito in a nudist camp — you know exactly what to do, but where do you start?

We began this project nearly eight years ago. It started when attendees at Pencom's popular service and sales training seminars began writing, calling and faxing us for a list of the aphorisms and metaphors we use throughout our lively presentations.

> **"All I know is that somebody, somewhere said it, or we wouldn't print it."**
> Joe Flaherty
> as Guy Caballero on SCTV

A second stage of this book began when we asked our audiences to contribute their favorite quotes, sayings, thoughts and observations. The third piece of the puzzle developed after our best-selling book *Service That Sells!* was published and thousands of readers voluntarily sent in their one-liner perspectives on the art of profitable hospitality.

The final "chapter" of this book began when we published the first *Service That Sells! Newsletter* in 1993.

Every six weeks many of our 30,000 subscribers have been sending us their favorite quotes, quips and phrases. So what you see is what we got!

It's all here: from the familiar to the funky, including dozens of quotes that have never been printed anywhere before from "service gurus" to real business people who either manage, work in or own successful service-driven companies.

If your favorite isn't in this collection, and it should be, write it down and send it to Pencom at the address listed on the last page and we'll make certain that it's included in future editions, with credit to you.

Please note that all quotes attributed to *Service That Sells! The Art of Profitable Hospitality* are from the Pencom book of the same title ($16.95).

In closing, I'd like to quote Paul Dickson, who said, "If you had half as much fun reading this as I had compiling it, then I had twice as much fun as you!"

Read 'em and reap!

*Jim Sullivan*

Jim Sullivan
President
Pencom, Inc.

# WHAT CAN I LEARN FROM A QUOTEBOOK?

Naturally, writers love quote books. Finding the exact expression, insight or clever remark to punctuate an article, story or opinion is like adding the sizzle to the steak. But how can those of us who are not writers use a quote book to elicit more than a chuckle or a knowing nod? How can business people, managers and front-line servers use a quote or a phrase to improve

*What they never told you in school: How to use a quote book to improve service or increase sales.*

performance, profits and productivity? Good question, and we're glad we asked it! Quotes can be extremely effective in accentuating training sessions, lesson plans or meetings in addition to providing life lessons for the rest of us. For instance, let's say you've just completed a training seminar, and maybe you want to reinforce the importance of your staff not only understanding but also using the new skills you have just taught them. Pull the quote from page 34: "If you always do what you always did, you always get what you always got," and

put it on your flip chart, overhead or handouts. You might tell your audience: "This quote stresses the importance of breaking old habits to provide better service. So now, let's list some of the barriers we may have in our system or behavior that inhibit better service delivery." Ask your associates to interpret the quotes you choose and encourage the shared insight that participation brings. Then ask them for a commitment to *use* the knowledge or training that the quote has underscored. Then, always follow up to ensure that your staff is using the new behavior they've committed themselves to try. "Well done is better than well said" and "actions speak louder than words."

**Ready? Let's go!**

# SOURCES,
## REFERENCES
## and TRACKING
## THE WILD
## QUOTE

Attributing a specific remark to a particular person is difficult at best. We have thoroughly researched all sources to reasonably ensure the accuracy of the information in this book. In researching this collection we often found the same quote or idea attributed to a variety of different people, in many cases over two centuries. If you know of a speaker, author or source that we have failed to give proper credit to, call or write us at Pencom and we will immediately correct it in the next edition. We assume no responsibility for errors, inaccuracies or omissions. Any slights of quotable people or authors are unintentional and every attempt will be made to rectify any oversights in future editions. And, there's one last thing we'd like to say:

## Thank you!

# ACKNOWLEDGEMENTS

A good book is the result of a great team effort. Space limitations result in our not being able to thank everyone who contributed to this tome, nor can we acknowledge every individual who sent us a quote that we, unfortunately, were unable to use. But we would like to extend a big thanks and a tip 'o the Pencom hat to:

Jan Carlzon
Zig Ziglar
John Martin
Joe Micatrotto
Ron Magruder
Zoom Roberts
Tom Rector
Andy Seymour
Kelli Rehder
Erin Davis
Kristen Loop
Steve Hawkins

Charlie Haviland
Bill Walsh
Teri Merbach
Marvina Richardson
Pat Baird
Karen Brennan
John Keener
Bill Asbury
A.J. Edelstein
Gus Dussin
John Zehnder
Joe Norton

Wes Curl
Hap Herndon
Mike McMahon
Jim Samuel
Stan Novack
Paul White
Al Wheeler
Darrel Rolph
Steve Pettise
Richard Zdyb
Mike Plunkett

Service

In every service opportunity, there's a sales opportunity, and in every sales opportunity, there's a service opportunity.

*Jan Rusch, Zehnder's Restaurant, Frankenmuth, MI*

Whenever you dance with the customer, always let them lead.

*Manny Garcia, Florida restaurateur*

Because I wanted to be in a business where the customer is always wrong.

*Former waiter Brian Dilling, on why he became a policeman, 1991*

If you're going to teach a bear to dance, you've got to be prepared to keep dancing until the bear is ready to stop. The road to service excellence takes committed drivers.

*Benny Ball, Shoney's Restaurants*

Good service can save a bad meal.
A good meal cannot save bad service.
*Doug Roth, Chicago Restaurateur*


Make sure the story isn't better than the store.
*L.L. Bean*


The Five Steps of Service Excellence: Look at me. Smile at me.
Talk to me. Listen to me. Thank me.
*Training Manual, Brown Derby Restaurant, 1946*

We are not in business to break even, and neither are our customers. Every guest leaves our restaurants with a "mental profit and loss statement." Our challenge is to make sure that the mental profit column is high and the loss column is zero. Customers always review their "mental P & L" when deciding if they'll come back to our restaurant or go to the competition.

*Ron Magruder, President, Olive Garden Restaurants*

I can think of no company that has found a way
to look after external customers while abusing
internal customers. The process of meeting
customer needs begins internally.

Tom Peters, Author

If people want to call me Murph, let
them. It's important to be flexible in
this business.

Ed Hawkins, Owner, Murph's Restaurant, Franklin Square, New York

Don't fight. Make it right.
*Hardee's complaint-handling policy*

One of the surest signs of a bad or declining
relationship with a customer is the absence
of complaints. Nobody is that satisfied — especially
not over an extended period of time. The customer
is either not being candid or not being contacted.
*Theodore Levitt, Harvard University*

Foodservice will thrive only as long as the service outlasts the food.
*Greg Ibsen, VP Marketing, Specialty Brands*

We view "Going the Extra Mile" service as
an honor – not an obligation.

*Hal Stringer, President, Peerless Systems, Inc.*

It's not the thousand dollar thing that upsets the customer, but the five buck things that bug them.

*Earl Fletcher, Sales and Management Trainer, Volkswagen Canada*

You don't improve service and quality in general. You improve service and quality in specific.

*Dr. Rodney Dueck, Park Nicollet Centers, Minneapolis, MN*

Use your good judgement in all situations.
There will be no additional rules.

*Nordstrom, Inc. Employee Handbook*

If you're not serving the guest directly,
you'd better be serving someone who is.

*Jan Carlzon, CEO, Scandinavian Airline Systems*

Bad service happens all by itself;
good service has to be managed.

*Karl Albrecht*

What really counts is what they say
when they pull out of the driveway.

*Ann Sullivan*

Why go out and pay for bad service when you can
stay home and get it for free?
*Kevin Knee, VP Marketing, EMI Records Group*

There are 3 things to remember
about customer service:
1. Customer Perception
2. Customer Perception
3. Customer Perception
*Steve Phillips, Phillips Seafood*

We are the only business whose assets
walk out the door every day.

*Samuel Goldwyn, Movie Mogul*

Service quick is service best; unoccupied time
passes slower than occupied time.

*Service That Sells! The Art of Profitable Hospitality*

Never leave the kitchen or go into the dining room
empty-handed: full hands in, full hands out.

*Motto, Brinker International*

Restaurant Server Tip #1: It is not how much you make a night, it is
how much you wake up with in the morning.

*John Keener & Joe Norton, Owners, Charleston Crab House, J. J. Hooks*

A "consumer" is a shopper who is sore about something.

Harold Glen Coffin

If you strive to be 1% better every day, how much better will you be in 100 days?

Larry Griewisch, Co-owner, VP, Jackson's Hole Sports Grills

We do pea soup well and we make the most out of that.

Ray Benitez, Pea Soup Anderson's, Buellton, CA

This is not Burger King! We do not do it your way.
This is the county jail. You will do it our way.
*Sign in Chicago's Cook County Jail cafeteria*

Platinum rule: Treat customers the way they want to
be treated; not the way you want to be treated.
*Jim Cathcart*

The secret to restaurant success?
Details, details, details.
*Gus Dussin, President, Old Spaghetti Factory*

Share and share alike really means
to care about each other's likes.
*Al Wheeler, Division VP Sales, Nestle Brands*

The customer is not always right, but treat them as though they
are — this keeps you sane and them happy!
*Joseph P. Micatrotto, President, CEO, Chi-Chi's Mexican Restaurants*

The customer is not always right, but the customer is always the
customer, and it's alright for the customer to be wrong.
*Tom Rector, VP Direct Sales, Specialty Brands*

The point of these contests and recognition programs and service evaluations and checklists is that they make everyone feel that service is his or her individual responsibility. That not only leads to better service quality for the customer, it also means higher morale.

*Lauren O'Connel, Citicorp*

Every single customer is a "secret" shopper.

*Gus Dussin, President, Old Spaghetti Factory*

The sunnier the weather
– the sicker the staff.
*John Zehnder, Food & Beverage Director, Zehnder's Restaurant*

The function of your business is to
acquire and maintain customers.
The goal is to make money.
*Phil Wexler, Trainer*

All the world's a stage but
a restaurant is Broadway.
*Hap Herndon, Director of Training, Brinker International*

Two men were laying brick.
The first was asked,
"What are you doing?"
He answered, "Laying some brick."
"What are you working for?"
He answered, "Five dollars a day."

The second man was asked, "What
are you doing?"
He answered, "I am helping to
build a great Cathedral."

Which man are you?
*Charles Schwab*

For us it may be just another meal,
but for our customers it's always a special occasion.

*Sign in the kitchen of White Fence Farm, Lakewood, CO*

Ninety percent of all businesses do 90% of the same things the same
way. It's the 10% you do differently that spells success.

*James C. Doherty, Publisher*

Eighty percent of the customers' problems are caused
by bad systems, not bad people.

*John Goodman, President, Tarp Inc.*

Change with the times or the times will change you.
*Fry Cook, Gary's Duck Restaurant, Orlando, 1990*

It's a mistake to believe that you have to pay for quality. You are entitled to quality, whatever you pay.
*Bob Snyder, G & S Enterprises*

Great marketing can kill a bad business.
*Dan Dains, Colorado Restaurateur*

When one is helping another, both are strong.
*German proverb*

Quality is the first thing seen.
Service is the first thing felt.
Price is the first thing forgotten.
*Bonanza Restaurants training manual*

Always under-promise and over-deliver.
*Carol Sewell*

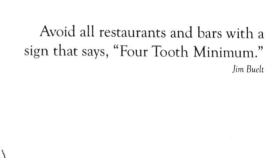

Avoid all restaurants and bars with a
sign that says, "Four Tooth Minimum."
*Jim Buelt*

Service "gurus" are like diapers. You need to change them a lot and for the same reasons.
*Jim Sullivan*

I was once in a restaurant so bad that four empty seats got up and walked out.
*Tom Koch, Pizza Hut, Inc.*

It's a lot easier to explain higher prices than poor quality.
*Andy Seymour, Vice President, Pierce Foods*

You cannot be 100% better than your competition. Try to be 1% better in a hundred different ways.
*Service That Sells! The Art of Profitable Hospitality*

Our best salesperson is an 85 degree sunny day.
*Beer Salesman John McQueeney, 1993*

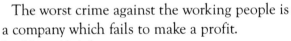

Happy customers buy more.
*Ron Magruder, President, Olive Garden Restaurants*

The worst crime against the working people is a company which fails to make a profit.
*Samuel Gompers, labor leader*

Man must sit for very long time with mouth open before roast duck fly in.

Sam Wo, Legendary San Francisco Restaurateur

You can have the best product in the world, but if you can't sell it, you've still got it!

Restaurateur "Diamond" Jim Brady, 1901

Everyone lives by selling something.

Robert Louis Stevenson

To sell is to serve, to serve is to sell.
*Service That Sells! The Art of Profitable Hospitality*

Every crowd has a silver lining.
*P.T. Barnum*

Nothing ever happens until
somebody sells something.
*Richard M. White, Jr., The Entrepreneur's Manual, 1977*

There is no such thing as "soft sell" and "hard sell."
There's only "smart sell" and "stupid sell."
*Charles Brower, news summaries, May 20, 1958*

People buy what they want when
they want it more than they
want the money it costs.
*Zig Ziglar, Secrets of Closing the Sale, 1984*

Babe Ruth hit 714 home runs in his career.
He also struck out 1,330 times.

*Graffiti*

Moral:
Be consistent in your sales
presentations and brave
enough to fail.

Help me to money and I'll help myself to friends.

*Thomas Fuller, Gnomologia, 1732*

People don't buy products, they buy solutions.

*Bill Sutphen, Kraft Foodservice, 1993*

Value is not low pricing, it is a quality product at
a fair price combined with excellent service.

*Stan Novack, VP Beverage Products & Concepts, Host·Marriott*

The fox that waited for the chickens to fall off their perch died of hunger.
*English Proverb*

44

The harder it is to read the menu,
the higher the prices on it.
*Kelli Rehder*

Your "competition" is not your competition. Your competition is the competency level of your salespeople.
*Tom Peters*

In God we trust, all others pay cash.
*Sign in an Arkansas diner*

A horse standing in a field chomping on grass does not constitute one horse power.
*Mark Twain*

People don't buy what it is,
they own what it does.
*Bill Asbury*

Selling is helping people
make a decision that's
good for them.
*Service That Sells! The Art of Profitable Hospitality*

IF YOU DON'T BUY THIS MAGAZINE,
WE'LL KILL THIS DOG.

*January 1973 cover of National Lampoon*

Money can't buy friends,
but you can get a better class of enemy.
*Spike Milligan*

People don't want to make a million dollars,
they want to spend it.
*Darrel Rolph, President, Sasnak Management Company*

A salesperson is someone who sells goods that won't
come back to customers who will.
*Anonymous*

There are only salespeople
and order-takers. Salespeople
serve. Order-takers are walking,
talking, vending machines.
*Service That Sells! The Art of Profitable Hospitality*

Money won't buy happiness,
but it will pay the salaries of a
large research staff to study why
poverty saddens people so.
*Anonymous*

Ten percent of something is
better than ten percent of nothing.
*Randy Anderson (a former waiter on the good fortune
of being able to serve guests regardless of how they tip)*

Value is not what people pay for something, value is what they get in exchange for their money.

*Service That Sells! The Art of Profitable Hospitality*

I don't care a damn for the invention. The dimes are what I'm after.

*Issac Singer on his sewing machine*

Anything that won't sell, I don't want to invent.

*Thomas Edison*

A well-informed employee is the best
salesperson a company can have.
*Edwin J. Thomas*

I am the world's worst salesman,
therefore I must make it easy
for people to buy.
*Frank W. Woolworth*

The most expensive thing in a
restaurant is an empty chair.
*Cris Roshko, Toronto Restaurateur*

You miss 100% of the shots you never take.

*Wayne Gretzky*

Training

If you try to save money on training, you end up spending twice as much on advertising.

*John Martin, President and CEO, Taco Bell Corp.*

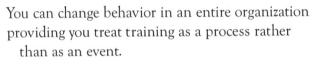

You can change behavior in an entire organization providing you treat training as a process rather than as an event.

*Edward Jones, General Cinema Beverages, Inc.*

What if you train your servers to sell and they leave? What if you don't and they stay?

*Brad Huisken*

A baseball swing is a very finely tuned instrument.
It is repetition and more repetition, then a little more
after that.

*Reggie Jackson, Baseball Hall of Famer*

*Moral:* Train daily, daily, daily. Then train some more.

A well-placed "well done" is the most powerful motivator a manager has and the least used.
*Thomas Connelan, How to Grow People Into Self Starters*

Nothing worth learning is learned quickly except parachuting.
*George Feeney*

Consider the postage stamp: its usefulness consists of its ability to stick to one thing until it gets there.
*Henry Wheeler Shaw*

Repetition is the motor of learning.
*Chuck Chapman, General Mills Restaurants*

The expense of training isn't what it costs to train employees. It's what it costs not to train them.
*Philip Wilber, President, Drug Emporium, Inc.*

An employee is never more focused, malleable, and teachable than the first day on the job.
*Horst Schulze, CEO, Ritz-Carlton Hotels*

Training is a philosophy, not a department.
*Liza Mason, G.M., Marlowe's Restaurant, Denver, CO*

No train? No gain.

*Service That Sells! The Art of Profitable Hospitality*

Train daily. What you reinforce is what you get.
What you don't reinforce is what you lose.

*Tom Peters*

You can take great people, highly trained
and motivated, and put them in a lousy
system and the system will win every time.

*Geary Rummler, President, The Rummler-Bache Group*

If you think training is expensive, try ignorance.

*Service That Sells! The Art of Profitable Hospitality*

All manuals are out of date.

*Unknown*

"Deja vu" is only poor memory; you have done it before.
*Jim Buelt*

The more you expect from a person, the more you have to train them.
*Geoff Bailey, Colorado Restaurateur*

Train today for tomorrow. It wasn't raining when Noah built the ark.
*Howard Ruff*

You were not hired, you were selected.
*Jim Veil, General Manager, Ritz-Carlton, to new employees*

Habit is habit and not to be flung out of the window by any man but coaxed downstairs a step at a time.
*Mark Twain*

Employees can't be empowered until you train them.
*Paul Kazarian*

It takes 21 days of different behavior to break a habit.
*Weight Watchers*

The greatest enemy of training in the classroom is preoccupation or distraction. The greatest enemy of training outside the classroom is habit.

*Bob Pike*

You don't hire people, you rent behavior.

*W. Steven Braun*

First prize is the El Dorado,
second prize is the steak knives.
Third is, you're fired.

*Incentive program from the film Glengarry Glen Ross*

Success isn't how far you've gotten, it's the distance you traveled from where you started. Be patient, but persistent, with sales training. Fall seven times, stand up eight.

*Service That Sells! The Art of Profitable Hospitality*

Creative minds have always been known to survive any kind of training.

*Anna Freud (1895-1982), Austrian psychoanalyst*

Remember: the ears have walls.

*Mike Amos, Tucson Restaurateur*

It is a pity to shoot the pianist when the piano is out of tune.

*René Coty*

Before the squeaky wheel gets the grease, check first
to see if it isn't just spinning.
*Graffiti*

Always invest in your greatest resource: your employees. Like the
Japanese proverb says: If they work for you, you work for them.
*Service That Sells! The Art of Profitable Hospitality*

An informed soldier fights best.

*US Army Orientation booklet, WWII*

If you train your salespeople they will do what they fear most.

*Tom Hopkins*

Is management's unwillingness to train daily caused by ignorance or apathy? I don't know and I don't care.

*Michael Feeney*

What we've got here is a failure to communicate.

*Strother Martin in* Cool Hand Luke

As we say in the sewer, if you're not prepared to go all the way,
don't put your boots on in the first place.

*Ed Norton, The Honeymooners*

The game is scheduled. We have to play. We might as well win it.
*Bill Russell, coach*

If you always do what you always did, you always get what you always got.
*Service That Sells! The Art of Profitable Hospitality*

Why didn't you hit a home run like I told you to? If you're not going to do what I tell you, what's the use of my being a manager?
*Groucho Marx to Jack Benny in a charity softball game*

Seek first to understand,
then to be understood.
*Stephen Covey, author*

When you hear employee A
criticize employee B, you learn
more about employee A than
you learn about employee B.
*Service That Sells! The Art of Profitable Hospitality*

You're hired by the people you
report to and fired by the people
who report to you.
*Service That Sells! The Art of Profitable Hospitality*

The higher up in the organization a person is, the more befuddled they are at the copy machine.

*Unknown*

71

Understanding how to operate a successful restaurant is a lot like having a hangover; until you actually experience it, you just don't know what it's like.

*Diamond Jim Brady, circa 1902*

Don't tell me about the labor pains.
Show me the baby.

*Johnny Sain, pitcher*

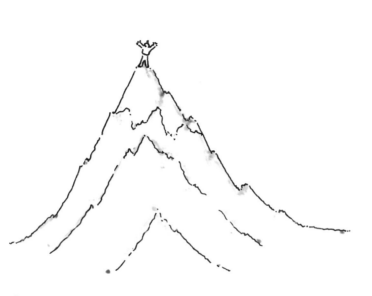

The person on the top of the mountain didn't fall there.
*Tom Lackmann, Lackmann Foodservices*

If he gossips to you, he'll gossip about you.
*Jay Barack*

Different is not always better:
but better is always different.
*Service That Sells! The Art of Profitable Hospitality*

The race is not always to the swift,
nor the battle to the strong,
but that's the way to bet.
*Damon Runyon*

Like my old skleenball coach used to say,
"Find out what you don't do well, and don't do it."

*Alf*

The harder you work the luckier you get.

*Gary Player, golfer*

You have to keep busy. After all, a dog's never
peed on a moving car. Know what I mean?

*Tom Waits*

It's not enough to be busy ... the question is: What are we busy about?

Henry David Thoreau


When I hear somebody sigh that "Life is hard," I am always tempted to ask, "Compared to what?"

Sydney Harris


Remember that a kick in the ass is a step forward.

John Kucera

When hiring, do you interview 27 people
to find the right person? Or do you interview
only once and hire the same person 27 times?
*Len Schlesinger, Harvard Professor*

I knew we were in for a long season when
we lined up for the national anthem on
opening day and one of my players said,
"Every time I hear that song I have a bad game."
*Jim Leyland, Baseball Manager*

You can't tell how far a frog can
jump by just looking at it.
*Moultre Hale Cornelius III, Texas Restaurateur*

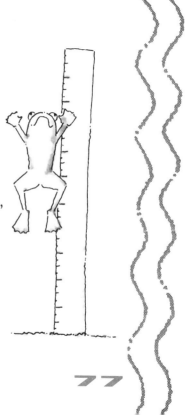

77

You can't build a reputation
on what you're *going* to do.
Henry Ford

If you have to kiss a toad — don't spend a whole lotta time looking at it.
Larry Griewisch, Co-owner, VP, Jackson's Hole Sports Grills

Too bad all the people who know how to run the country are busy driving taxi cabs and cutting hair.
*George Burns*

For every "will" there's a "won't."
*Ken Boulay*

79

A pat on the back is just a few vertebrae up from a kick in the ass.

*Service That Sells! The Art of Profitable Hospitality*

You only have to do 20% of your job if you do the 20%
of the job that makes 80% of the difference.

*Karen Brennan, VP Marketing, Max & Erma's Restaurant, Inc.*

Rule #1: Don't sweat the small stuff.
Rule #2: When managed well, it's all small stuff.

*Jan Whitmire, Director of Corporate Development, Brinker International*

I have a simple philosophy. Fill what's empty. Empty what's full. Scratch where it itches.
*Alice Roosevelt Longworth.*

The difference between genius and stupidity is that genius has its limits.
*Brian Rehder*

My brother-in-law works at the same restaurant I do — he's the anchor man. We call him that because he keeps us from moving forward.

*Arizona restaurateur who prefers to remain anonymous*

Managing is gettin' paid for home runs that someone else hits.

*Casey Stengel*

"I must do something" will solve more problems than "something must be done."

*Roxanne K. Pishnick, Director Government Relations, T.G.I. Friday's*

If you wait until something is broken to fix it, there may not be anything left to fix!

*John E. Martin, President & CEO, Taco Bell Corp.*

Accomplishing the impossible means only that the boss will then assign it to your regular duties.

*Doug Larson*

Motivation is like bathing — it may not last, but it's still a good idea now and then.

*Jim Cathcart*

It ain't bragging if you done it.
*Dizzy Dean*

You don't try to build character in a team, you
eliminate people who don't have character.
*Paul Brown, Cleveland Browns founder*

A coach is someone who makes you do what you don't want to do so
you can be who you always wanted to be.
*Tom Landry*

If you want to give a man credit, put it in writing.
If you want to give him hell, do it on the phone.

*Charlie Blacham (Iacocoa's mentor)*

When the going gets tough, the weird
turn pro!

*Rick Nelson*

Show-how is better than know-how.

*Dick Credenza*

What gets rewarded gets
repeated.

*Tom Peters*

Plan your work and work your plan.

*Anonymous*


A consultant is someone who tells you 1,001 ways to make love,
but doesn't know any women.

*Don Goetz*


The secret to operating a successful nightclub: "Get 'em Up,
Get 'em Thirsty, Set 'em Down, Let 'em Drink!"

*Clint Hughes, VP Strategic Marketing & National Accounts,*
*Harborage I, LTD*

My idea of discipline is not makin' guys do something, it's gettin' 'em to do it. There's a difference in bitchin' and coachin'.
*Bum Phillips*

Be disciplined and strict early; it's easier to get soft with people later on than it is to get hard with them.
*William J. Walsh, Jr., President, Daland Corporation*

Nothing makes a person more productive than the last minute.
*Fry cook, Shoney's Restaurant, St. Louis. MO*

Critics are like eunuchs in a harem: they know how it's done, they've seen it done every day, but they're unable to do it themselves.
*Brendan Behan*

If you do it then it's done.
*Proverb*

If you chase two rabbits, both will escape.
*Russian proverb*

The function of every employee is to be an ass<u>et</u>, not an ass----!
*Lance Heckel*

I hate to advocate drugs, alcohol, violence or insanity to anyone,
but they've always worked for me.
*Hunter S. Thompson*

Monkeys are superior to men in this: when a monkey looks into a mirror, he sees a monkey.

Malcolm de Chazal

Want to build character in our youth? Every young American should be required to spend two years in military service or two years in the hospitality business!

Maureen Costello, Regional National Account Manager, Brown-Forman Beverage Company

Pay peanuts and you get monkeys.

Anonymous

Why is it that there are so many more
horses' asses than there are horses?
*G. Gordon Liddy*

Man is the only animal that laughs
and has a state legislature.
*Samuel Butler*

Rotten wood cannot be saved.
*Chinese Proverb*

It's important that people know what you stand for. It's equally important that they know what you won't stand for.

*Mary Waldrip*

If some people got their rights, they would complain of being deprived of their wrongs.

*Oliver Herefond*

In baseball, as in business, a game won today will count as much as a game won at the end of the season.
*Johnny Bench*

Nobody roots for Goliath.
*Wilt Chamberlain, very tall guy*

BOO!

A government that robs Peter to pay Paul can always depend on the support of Paul.
*George Bernard Shaw*

God gives the nuts, but does not crack them.
*Proverb*

Business is more than making money; losing less money is sometimes important, too.
*Kim Woo-Choong, Every Street is Paved With Gold*

You can't talk your way out of what you've behaved yourself into.
*A.J. Edelstein, Regional Director of Operations, Harborage I, Inc.*

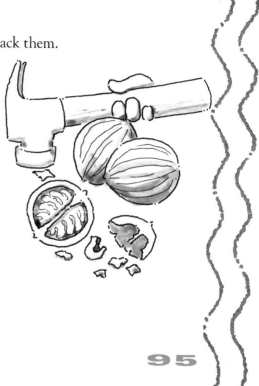

Don't buy a $10,000 solid gold sledge hammer to drive in a two-cent thumb tack.

John Bear

Be specific. Work always fills the time allotted for it.

John Zehnder, Food & Beverage Director, Zehnder's Restaurant

Twenty-five cents of every twenty-nine-cent stamp goes for storage.

Louis Rukeyser

Managers are rewarded not for
what they do but for what their people do.
*Service That Sells! The Art of Profitable Hospitality*

To keep an organization young and fit, don't
hire anyone until everybody's so overworked
they'll be glad to see the newcomer no matter
where he sits.
*Robert Townsend, Further Up the Organization, 1984*

When an employee tells you it's the principle of
the thing and not the money, it's the money.
*Jean Goetz*

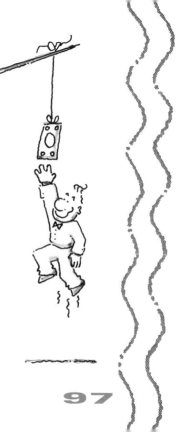

If you hear that everyone is buying a certain stock, ask who is selling.
*Andy Roberts*

If the house is on fire, forget the china, silver, and wedding album — grab the Rolodex.
*Harvey MacKay*

Don't expect. Inspect.
*Anonymous*

The best person you interview isn't necessarily the best person for the job.
*Robert Half, Robert Half on Hiring, 1985*

How can I have so much bad luck with four horseshoes?
*TV horse, Mr. Ed*

To get to the top of the heap, first you must have a heap.

Gene Perret

If you think you've heard every excuse in the book,
wait until tomorrow.

*John Zehnder, Food & Beverage Director, Zehnder's Restaurant*

Surround yourself with the highest caliber people. Remember that
first rate people hire first rate people — while second rate people hire
third rate people.

*Richard M. White, Jr., The Entrepreneur's Manual, 1977*

It's not what you pay a man but what he costs you that counts.

*Will Rogers, quoted by Richard M. Ketchum, Will Rogers, His Life and Times, 1973*

Any day you don't learn something new
you're just not paying attention.
*Mike Plunkett, Regional Manager, Dave & Buster's*

If you can't change your people,
then you must change your people.
*Tom Hopkins*

Go as far as you can see and when
you get there you will see farther.
*Early American Proverb*

The pursuit of excellence is a higher
calling than its achievement.
*Joseph P. Micatrotto, President, CEO, Panda Restaurants*

If we're all thinking alike, somebody isn't thinking.

*General George Patton*

Negotiating is like making love. A lot of it's in your head, you have to set the mood, know your partner, both parties have to be satisfied ... and you can't rush the outcome.

*Helen Moskovitz*

It is wise to remember that you are one of those people who can be fooled some of the time.

*Paul Beninati*

The restaurant business is like dancing
with a tiger — when you're tired you can't sit down.

Richard Zdyb, President, Zebbs Restaurants, Inc.

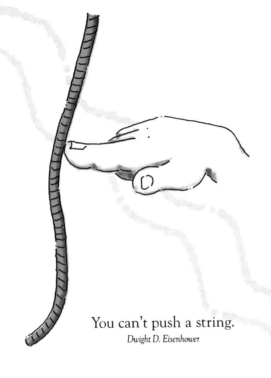

You can't push a string.

*Dwight D. Eisenhower*

First we will be best, and then we will be first.
*Grant Tinker*

The will to win is not as important as the will to prepare to win.
*Bobby Knight*

And so the time has come for us to unquo the status.
*Unknown*

Talk low, talk slow, and don't say too much.
*John Wayne*

People will accept your idea much more
readily if you tell them Benjamin Franklin said it.
*David Comins*

When in doubt, tell them Mark Twain said it.
*Layton "Mark Twain" Lyon*

Ben Franklin told me to tell you
to give me a hundred dollars. Oh,
and so did Mark Twain.
*Dick Credenza*

Never learn to do anything. If you don't learn,
you'll always find someone else to do it.
*Mark Twain*

I think it's a good idea.
*Coach John McKay, on what he thought of his team's execution*

If you cannot win, make the one ahead of you break the record.
*Jan McKeithen in Camden County, Georgia Tribune*

"Good enough" never is.
*Service That Sells! The Art of Profitable Hospitality*

Love 'em and lead 'em.

Javier Juarez, Denver restaurateur

If you are the boss and you stop rowing,
don't be surprised if everyone else stops rowing, too.

Steak and Ale Restaurant Manager, 1974

It takes as much courage to have tried and
failed as it does to have tried and succeeded.

Anne Morrow Lindbergh

No person was ever honored for what he received. Honor has been the reward for what they gave.

*Calvin Coolidge*

The best parachute folders are the ones who jump themselves.

*Dwight D. Eisenhower.*

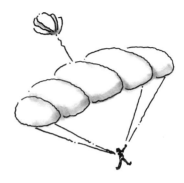

Teams tend to have leaders, leaders tend to create teams.

*Service That Sells! The Art of Profitable Hospitality*

Leadership is an affair of the heart as well as the head.

*Jim Kouzes*

Ready, fire, aim.
*Anonymous*

If at first you don't succeed,
you are running about average.
*M.H. Anderson*

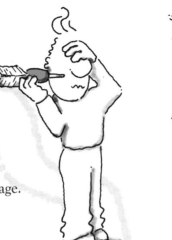

Everything has been thought of before,
but the problem is to think of it again.
*Goethe*

Progress involves risk. You can't steal
second base and keep your foot on first.
*Rick Van Warner, Magazine Editor*

The trouble with being a good sport
is that you have to lose in order to prove it.
*Moultre Hale Cornelius III*

Why am I always the leader? Cuz I'm
surrounded by nuthin' but knuckleheads.
*Moe Howard, Leader, the Three Stooges*

113

Do not follow the beaten path.
Go where there is no road and blaze a trail.

*Anonymous*

Drinking

They talk of my drinking
but never my thirst.
*Rodney Dangerfield*

'Twas a woman who drove me to
drink, and I never had the cour-
tesy to thank her for it.
*W.C. Fields*

A drunk will never spill
a drink on another drunk.
*Michael Gutstein*

I always wake up at the crack of ice.
*Joe E. Louis*

You mix two jiggers of scotch to one jigger of Slim Fast.
So far I've lost five pounds and my driver's license.

*Rocky Bridges on his diet*

Work is the curse of the drinking classes.

*Oscar Wilde*

Everybody should believe in something;
I believe I'll have another drink.

*Wilson Mizner, Los Angeles Restaurateur, 1938*

My old man was the town drunk.
And we lived in Chicago.
*Rodney Dangerfield*

Don't trust a brilliant idea unless
it survives the hangover.
*Jimmy Breslin*

When I feel athletic I go to a
sports bar.
*Rick Sullivan*

I've never been drunk, but I've often been overserved.
George Gobel

Remember, whiskey and gasoline don't mix. So please, please don't drink gasoline.
Pat O'Byrne

I haven't touched a drop of alcohol since the invention of the funnel.
Malachy McCourt

Sir, you speak the
language of my tribe.
*Buffalo Bill Cody's usual response to the offer of a free drink.*

If I'm *legally* drunk, then why are
you taking me to jail???
*Charlie Haviland*

Never cry over spilled milk.
It could have been whiskey.
*Pappy Maverick*

The sport of skiing consists of wearing three thousand dollars worth of clothes and equipment and driving two hundred miles in the snow in order to stand around at a bar and get drunk.

*P.J. O'Rourke*

Candy is dandy, but liquor is quicker.

*Ogden Nash*

It's easier to stand the smell of liquor than to listen to it.

*Grandpa Sullivan*

Song title: Don't Put On That Swim Suit Mother, It's Not That Kind Of Dive

*Unknown*

I have taken more out of alcohol than alcohol has taken out of me.

*Winston Churchill*

An Irishman is the only man in the world who will step over the bodies of naked women to get to a bottle of stout.

*Anonymous*

I never have more than one drink before dinner. But I do like that one to be large and very strong and very cold and very well-made.
*James Bond, Ian Fleming's Casino Royale*

Happiness is a hungry man finding two olives in his martini.
*Johnny Carson*

I feel sorry for anyone who doesn't drink. Every morning when they wake up they know that's the best they're gonna feel all day.

*Robert Mitchum*

**Q:** Hey, Norm, how does a beer sound?

**Norm:** Pretty quiet 'til four in the morning.

*Cheers*

Eating

In Mexico we have a word for sushi: bait.

*José Simon*

You are where you eat.
*Bob Garcia*

Fact: The seafood is always fresh, even in Utah.
*Bathroom graffiti in a Boston restaurant*

It is more fun to eat in a bar than it is to drink in a restaurant.
Zoom Roberts

"All You Can Eat" doesn't mean
"Take This Food and Shove It."
Wes Roberts

I am not a vegetarian because I love animals.
I'm a vegetarian because I hate plants.
A. Whitney Brown

I like airline food.

*Mel Turpin, professional basketball player,*
*explaining how he gained 17 pounds in one day on a road trip*

Life itself is the proper binge.

*Julia Child*

Seeing is deceiving.
It's eating that's believing.

*James Thurber*

Cannibal: a guy who goes into a restaurant and orders the waiter.
*Jack Benny*

The difference between a cook and a chef is the size of the mess.
*John Zehnder, Food & Beverage Director, Zehnder's Restaurant*

The tallest remedy for a quick temper is a short trip to the walk-in cooler.
*Darren Minich*

Do not make loon soup.

*Stark advice from The Eskimo Cookbook*

Never eat more than you can lift.

*Miss Piggy*

Part of the secret of success in life is to eat what you like and let the food fight it out inside.

*Mark Twain*

When my mother had to get dinner for eight she'd just make enough
for sixteen and only serve half.
Gracie Allen

Wish I had time for just one more bowl of chili.
Alleged dying words of Kit Carson

Tell me what you eat and
I will tell you what you are.
Brillat-Savarin

There's nothing wrong with cooks
that reasoning with them won't aggravate.
*Cathy Eck, Ohio Restaurateur*

If it fits on your plate,
it'll fit in your stomach.
*Steve O'Flaherty*

God sends meat and
the devil sends cooks.
*Thomas Delaney*

Cook #1: Didn't I tell you to notice when the soup boiled over?
Cook #2: I did. It was ten thirty.

*Two prep cooks in Marlowe's kitchen, 1993*

Music with dinner is an insult to both the cook and the violinist.

*G.K. Chesterton*

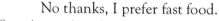

No thanks, I prefer fast food.

*Customer's rejection of a waiter's suggestion of snails as an appetizer*

Accidents will happen. That's why there are so many types of salad.

*Greg Phillips, Kansas Restaurateur*

Anyone who eats three meals a day should understand why cook-
books outsell sex books three to one.

*L.M. Boyd*

The smallest hole will eventually empty the largest container in a
restaurant, unless it was made intentionally for drainage,
in which case it will clog.

*Tito Mendez, Kitchen Manager*

Cleanliness is next to godliness except in the employee restroom,
where it is next to impossible.

*Kitchen Manager, Oklahoma City, 1994*

"          "

*Marcel Marceau*

Do you have a great quote that you're dying to share? Send it to us at:

Pencom, Inc.
Attention: Quotable Quotes
511 Sixteenth Street, Suite 400
Denver, CO 80202
Or fax it toll free to 1-800-746-2211

We'll credit you in the next edition and send you a free t-shirt if we use your quote. Please indicate the source of the quote if it's not an original.

*Thanks!*

**P.S.** The numerous quotes in this collection attributed to "Service That Sells!" are from the best selling book *Service That Sells! The Art of Profitable Hospitality* (Pencom Press, Denver, CO, $16.95). To order your copies, call toll-free:

# 1-800-247-8514

# OTHER PRODUCTS TO INCREASE YOUR PROFITS

This book is only one in a series of service and suggestive sales
training products available from Pencom, Inc.
Invest in these products as well.

# Books

*Service That Sells! The Art of Profitable Hospitality*

With this book, you and your entire staff will learn:

- How to raise guest checks $1 or more per person

- 101 ways to sell more appetizers

- 14 ways to reduce costs

- 31 ways to transform order-takers into salespeople

- 6 ways to motivate teen workers

- 12 ways to improve your neighborhood marketing

- 26 ways to improve your service

- And much more!

New edition — revised, expanded, and updated in 1994! 178 pages, illustrated, appendix.

*Work Smarter – Not Harder!*
*The Service That Sells Waitstaff Workbook*

This dynamic interactive workbook is
designed exclusively for waiters, waitresses and bartenders. They'll learn over
21 guaranteed ways to improve service,
increase sales and reduce costs. Based on
the principles detailed in our best-selling
book *Service that Sells!*, this fun-filled,
award-winning, interactive workbook will
make your current training manual
obsolete and transform your order-takers
into salespeople.

# Multiple Purchase Discounts Save You Big Bucks!

All of our books, including the one you're reading, are available at major discounts when you buy 10 or more. Call 1-800-247-8514.

# Videos

### Service That Sells! The Video

Putting it all together ... Managing our cycle of service. A complete program for the entire staff to maximize customer satisfaction and increase sales.

### 50 Ways to Manage Service That Sells!

If you've ever caught one of Pencom President Jim Sullivan's live seminars, you know why they're standing room only! Now bring Jim to your restaurant to train your staff any time with this video.

*CheckBusters: The Art of Smart Selling!*
What if you train your servers to sell and they
leave? What if you don't ... and they stay?!
You asked for it — a sales training video for
servers, bartenders, hosts and hostesses that
is realistic, relevant and *gets results*, instead of
merely "covering content" — so you got it,
*CheckBusters: The Art of Smart Selling!* As a
companion, interactive server workbooks are
also available.

# Increase
# Retention
## with
# Interactive
## Workbooks

Interactive Trainee Workbooks are available for most of our video programs for as low as $1 each. Call 1-800-247-8514.

## How To Sell More Beer

This fast and fun-paced 25-minute video will show your waiters, waitresses and bartenders how to sell more draft and bottled beer, how to trade up regular beer to super-premium brands, how to up-sell draft beers to pitchers, how to pair up appetizers with beer and how to sell more non-alcohol brews. Transform your order-takers into a real brew crew.

### How To Sell More Appetizers

What's the best way to increase check averages? Sell your customers appetizers, soups or salads. This fun and informative video and instructor guide (interactive workbooks also available) will show your host staff, servers and bartenders over 30 ways to increase your appetizer sales.

### How To Sell More Wine

This fun and fast-paced video and instructor guide will show your servers, managers and host staff how to double your wine sales, champagne sales and much, much more.

### How To Sell More Premium Spirits

This dynamic video and instructor guide will show you 10 sure-fire ways to increase your sales of premium spirits, including how to upgrade well drinks to premium brands, how to "assume the sale" of re-orders and how to increase drink sales through creative internal marketing.

# Audios

*Service That Sells! Live*

Our best-selling audio! The only place in America where you can get an audio recording of Jim Sullivan's award-winning *Service That Sells!* seminar. This two-tape program will teach your managers and servers:

- 5 ways to improve training
- 91 ways to increase sales
- How to train hosts and hostesses to sell
- 10 ways to increase business without advertising
- 12 ways to lower monthly costs
- How to increase your guest checks $1 per person

### Playing Games At Work

Once your staff is trained to better serve and sell, you'll need some practical ideas for effective server contests, rewards and incentives. That's what Jim Sullivan explains from A to Z in this award-winning audio. It's the perfect compliment to the *52 Best Incentives* book.

### Audio Soundtracks

Audio versions of most of our videos are available and perfect to send home with your staff for re-training.

# Newsletter

*The Service That Sells! Newsletter*

Get hundreds of new marketing, service, sales and training ideas in every issue like approximately 30,000 other restaurateurs do. You don't have time to check into what your colleagues (and your competitors) are doing to increase traffic, boost sales and train servers to sell. We do! In fact, *The Service That Sells! Newsletter* uses the best new ideas from successful restaurant, bar and hotel operators around the world. Each newsletter delivers dozens of proven ways you can increase your profits. Durable, three-ring binders are also available for storing your newsletters.

## What They Say is What You Get ...

*The Service That Sells! Newsletter* is a great reinforcement of the sales training we do with our service staff. What begins with the book continues with the newsletter to keep our server's guest focus fresh.
— *Nancy Donahue, Director of Training, T.G.I. Friday's*

*The Service That Sells! Newsletter* anticipates our needs and pitfalls. You use hot tips, graphics and common dollars and cents to mold us, scold us and motivate us, better than any magazine or newsletter on the market today!

— *Tom Love, Pepe's Mexican Restaurant*

# Suggestive Selling Posters

Now that you've taught your servers how to be salespeople, not order-takers, keep their newly learned sales skills top-of-mind with these colorful handy posters. Each poster contains tested and effective server sales dialogue for tableside use to suggestively sell and up-sell appetizers, sides, beer, wine, champagne, specialty drinks and premium brands. Each poster is 11 x 17 and laminated to withstand years of use and abuse. Only $6.95 each or five for $19.95.

# 100%
## Satisfaction
### Guaranteed

All of Pencom's products are backed by our 100% money-back guarantee. If you invest in a product that you're not absolutely satisfied with, you can send it back to us and we'll give you a full refund.

# We're standing by....

Our training consultants are standing by to answer your questions and to help you invest in training products that are guaranteed to increase your sales, improve your service and boost your profits. So what are you waiting for?

# Call 1-800-247-8514 today!

# Product Pricing

## (All prices FOB in Denver, subject to change)

### Books: Read 'em and reap!

| | | |
|---|---|---|
| PUB-513 | Service that Sells! The Art of Profitable Hospitality | $16.95 |
| PUB-518 | Say What? The 305 Best Things Ever Said About Service, Sales and Supervision | $9.95 |
| PUB-519 | Work Smarter, Not Harder! The Service That Sells Workbook    (minimum order of 10) | $7.95 |
| PUB-520 | The 52 Best Hospitality Incentives, Contests and Rewards | $19.95 |

### Videos: A picture is worth 1,000 words, a moving picture is worth 10,000!

| | | |
|---|---|---|
| TVC-20 | 50 Ways to Manage Service That Sells! | $99.00 |
| TVC-25 | Service That Sells! The Video | $99.00 |
| TVC-26 | CheckBusters: The Art of Smart Selling | $149.00 |
| TVC-27 | How to Sell More Beer | $99.00 |
| TVC-28 | How to Sell More Appetizers | $99.00 |
| TVC-29 | How to Sell More Wine | $99.00 |
| TVC-30 | How to Sell More Premium Spirits | $99.00 |

(Note: all video prices are for VHS format. For European PAL version, add $50)

## Audios: Use your car as a mobile university!

| | | |
|---|---|---|
| AUD-101 | Service That Sells! Live (2-tape set) | $19.95 |
| AUD-102 | Playing Games At Work | $11.95 |
| AUD-103 | Audio version of Service That Sells! The Video | $11.95 |
| AUD-104 | Audio version of CheckBusters: The Art of Smart Selling | $11.95 |
| AUD-105 | Audio version of How to Sell More Beer | $11.95 |
| AUD-106 | Audio version of How to Sell More Appetizers | $11.95 |
| AUD-107 | Audio version of How to Sell More Wine | $11.95 |
| AUD-108 | Audio version of How to Sell More Premium Spirits | $11.95 |

## Newsletter: News you can use!

| | | | |
|---|---|---|---|
| NL-101 | The Service That Sells! Newsletter | (1 year U.S. subscription) | $89.00 |
| | | (1 year Canadian subscription) | $129.00 |
| | | (1 year International subscription) | $149.00 |

## Call 1-800-247-8514 for information on super package prices and multiple purchase discounts!